SCHOLASTIC INC.
New York Toronto London Auckland Sydney

Snowballs

Lois Ehlert

For information regarding permission, write to
Harcourt Brace & Co., Orlando, FL 32887.

ISBN 0-590-06580-7

Copyright © 1995 by Lois Ehlert.
All rights reserved. Published by Scholastic Inc., 555
Broadway, New York, NY 10012,
by arrangement with Harcourt Brace & Co.
TRUMPET and the TRUMPET logo are registered
trademarks of Scholastic Inc.

12 11 10 9 8 7 6 5   8 9/9 0 1 2/0

Printed in the U.S.A.   08

First Scholastic printing, January 1997

Weather reports on the back cover are reprinted with
permission from the *Milwaukee Journal*.

Do you think birds know when it's going to snow?

I do.
The seeds
we left out
were almost
gone.

New snow
would soon
bury the rest.

We'd been waiting for a really big snow, saving good stuff in a sack. Finally it was a perfect snowball day.

We rolled
three snowballs
and made a
snow dad.

Added a
snow mom

and
a cool
snow
boy.

Made
a snow
girl

CLAIM CHECK
See Reverse Side
for Conditions

34-080

MKE
MILWAUKEE
Wisconsin

and a round snow baby.

Built our cat and to end the day,

made our dog, Spot.

I guess you know what happened when the sun came out.

Snow dad's shrinking.

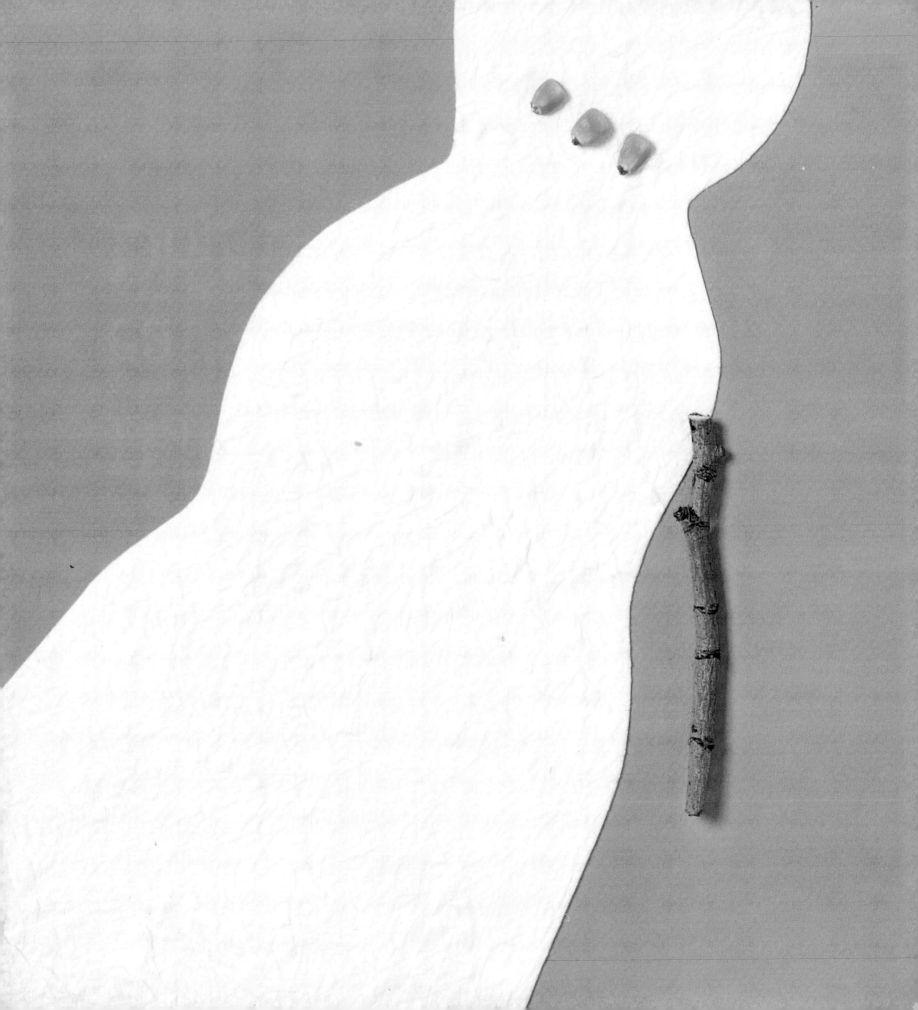

Mom is mush.
Boy's a blob;
girl is slush.

Baby's melting;
cat's getting small.
Dog is a puddle.

So long, snowball.

Guatemalan belt and tie

corn

fork

foil candy wrapper

walnut

bottle cap

button

Thai appliqué heart

evergreen branch

Mexican scrub brush

twig

Japanese stone

claim check

CLAIM CHECK
See Reverse Side
for Conditions

34-080

toy wheel

seashell

cinnamon stick

pencil

good stuff

pressed maple leaf

metal washer

toy fish

pine cone

Guatemalan purse

luggage tag

MKE
MILWAUKEE
Wisconsin

Bolivian hat

peanut

crayon

Made in U.S.A.
RED
NONTOXIC

strawberry

cranberry

African
kente cloth

screw

English
silk tie

Peruvian sock

telephone wire

metal nut

sunflower
seeds

coffee
bean

raisin

twine

ribbon

jingle
bell

popcorn

toy compass

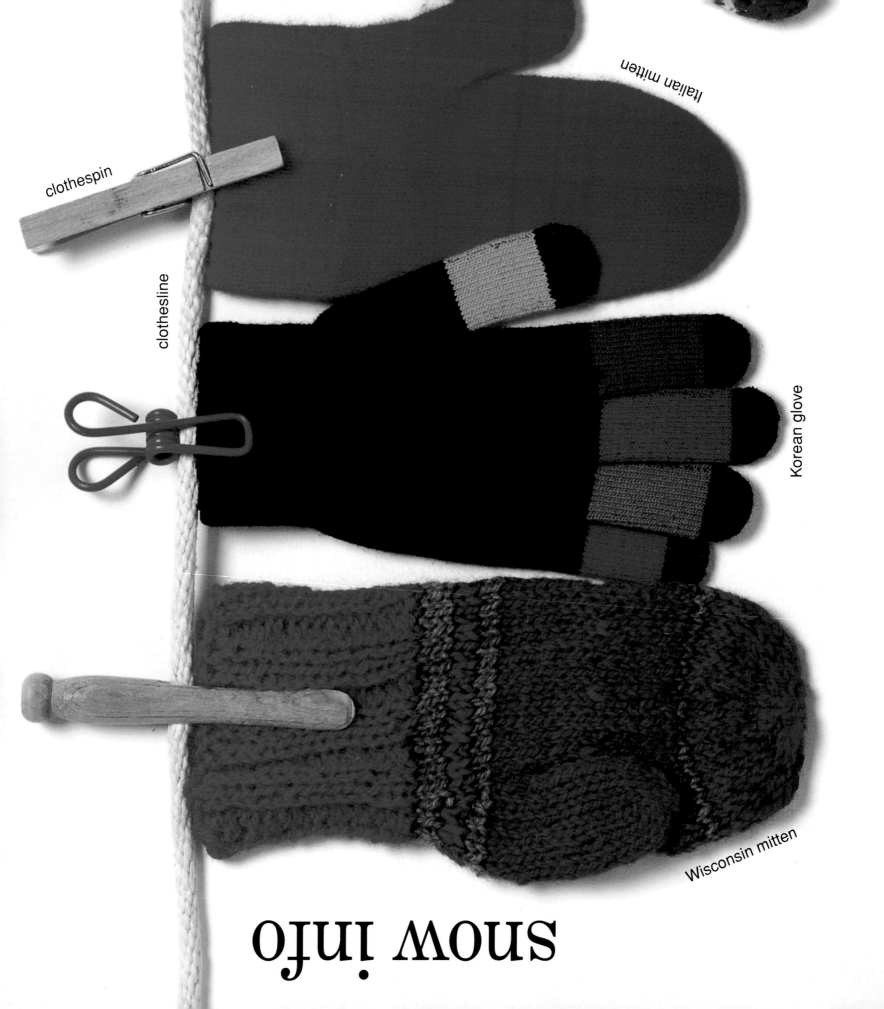

clothespin

Italian mitten

clothesline

Korean glove

Wisconsin mitten

snow info

Afghani glove

Wisconsin mitten

What is snow?

Snow is a frozen, solid form of water. Water can take three forms:

gas—droplets dispersed in air, such as steam or fog

liquid—rain, oceans, lakes, streams, rivers, and drinking water

solid—ice, snowflakes, hail, sleet, and frost

What makes it snow?

Although we can't always see the process, water is constantly evaporating from earth, changing from its liquid form to water vapor, its gas form. If you boil water, steam rises as gas. If your windows are cold, steam collects on the glass, cools, turns back into liquid, and water droplets run down your windows.

Imagine this process happening on a much larger scale. Water from our oceans, lakes, streams, and rivers evaporates, or turns into water vapor, which goes into the atmosphere. The water vapor blows around in the wind, clings to bits of dust and salt in the air, and gradually forms a cloud.

When a cloud becomes saturated with water vapor, it releases the droplets and water returns to earth. The temperature in the cloud determines whether it will release rain, snow, or other forms of precipitation, such as hail and sleet. If the cloud is warm, it will rain. If the temperature in the cloud is cold enough, water droplets freeze into ice crystals and snowflakes will fall. If the air below the cloud is warm, the snowflakes melt and fall as rain. If the air below is cool, the snow will continue its journey to earth.

If the earth is warm, snow melts when it lands. If it's cold, snow covers the ground, and that could mean a snowball day—at least until the warm sun comes out and melts the snow. Then the process of evaporation begins all over again.

Photographs are by Lillian Schultz except the three at the far right of this page, which are by Richard Ehlert, and the ones at the top and bottom left of this page, which are by Allyn Johnston.